A Passion
for Christ

CWR

Michael Baughen

© CWR 2019

Published 2019 by CWR, Waverley Abbey House, Waverley Lane, Farnham, Surrey GU9 8EP, UK. CWR is a Registered Charity – Number 294387 and a Limited Company registered in England – Registration Number 1990308.

The right of Michael Baughen to his own writings has been asserted by him in accordance with the Copyright, Designs and Patents Act 1988, sections 77 and 78.

See back of book for list of National Distributors.

Scripture references are taken from The Holy Bible, New International Version® Anglicised, NIV® Copyright © 1979, 1984, 2011 by Biblica, Inc.® Used by permission. All rights reserved worldwide.

Concept development, editing, design and production by CWR.

Every effort has been made to ensure that this book contains the correct permissions and references, but if anything has been inadvertently overlooked the Publisher will be pleased to make the necessary arrangements at the first opportunity. Please contact the Publisher directly.

Cover image: Adobestock

Printed in the UK by Linney.

ISBN: 978-1-78259-936-4

Contents

Introduction

Paul's life was fired by passion. He was passionate for Christ, for knowing Christ, for the gospel of Christ, for the Church of Christ and for everyone to follow and serve Christ. Mission was his top priority, even if this meant facing hardships and sorrows. His own personal comfort was of secondary importance. Paul followed his Lord – who walked the difficult path to Calvary – with utter devotion but also with much suffering.

This Lent, let's stand at the foot of the cross, gaze with our spiritual eyes on our Saviour and remember with amazement that 'we share abundantly in the sufferings of Christ' (2 Cor. 1:5). *We* share? How can this be? What does it entail? What does it mean for us? Why should it be so? How should this affect our own attitudes? In our studies, we will see how Paul brings the Passion of Christ and His sufferings right into our Christian lives, into our motivation, into our servanthood and into the depths of our soul.

Paul in his passionate letters to the Corinthians tackles their view that suffering is incompatible with true Christian living, and aims to clear up problems that had arisen in this area. For him, the sufferings of Christ for our salvation were a wonder of divine grace – that the Son of God would lower Himself to such agony and to the depths of the cross for us. As a devout Pharisee in his earlier days, Paul would be familiar with the verses in Scripture where Isaiah refers to the Messiah as 'my servant' (Isa. 52:13) and spells out all the sufferings He will undergo: 'surely he took up our pain and bore our suffering... he was pierced for our transgressions' (Isa. 53:4,5). In the aftermath of Christ's death and resurrection, these passages inevitably took on greater significance and explained why He had to go through such pain and agony.

Can we identify with Christ's sufferings? The Corinthians certainly didn't. But Paul saw through this and discerned something superficial. He wrote that the church had been infiltrated by 'false apostles, deceitful workers' (2 Cor. 11:13) who had the nerve to denigrate the great apostle Paul as 'unimpressive' and say that 'his speaking amounts to nothing' (10:10)! Paul addressed these criticisms head on: 'I may indeed be untrained as a speaker, but I do have knowledge' (11:6). Here was a man who had received a thorough training and was, as we know, theologically a giant for God, but the Corinthians were attracted to new 'teachers' and seemed to disregard anyone who suffered. As this included Paul, they turned against him and pronounced him unfit to be called an apostle.

This lack of compassion for those who suffer is also very contemporary. Although most people sympathise with those who struggle with long-term illness or disability, there are those who say that *everyone* can be healed and if you are not, then there is something wrong with your faith or you have hidden sin. The additional pain caused to many faithful believers by such statements is appalling, especially if it is said to a grieving parent.

The false prophets would, no doubt, have proudly listed their academic or social achievements. Paul, however, humbly listed his sufferings (2 Cor. 11:16–33) as his curriculum vitae! Like his Lord, he had suffered physically and been on the receiving end of abuse, humiliation and mockery, not because of any lack of faith but because of his passion to serve Christ: 'I do not think I am in the least inferior to those "super-apostles"' (v5).

In addition to all this, Paul wrote about a 'thorn in my flesh' (2 Cor. 12:7). We don't know what it was; it may have been a migraine or failing eyesight. ('Flesh' indicates the body and 'thorn' indicates something that happens to us, not by our action.) He pleaded three times in prayer that God would 'take it away from me' (v8). Was that in a day, over a week, a month or year? Again, we don't know, but clearly they were special times of prayer. Then comes the quiet assurance in Paul's heart that healing is not going to be God's way, and he received the words that have become precious to so many believers: 'My grace is sufficient for you, for my power is made perfect in weakness' (v9).

Instead of grudgingly putting up with his lot, Paul turned his suffering around to stir up fresh passion in himself for Christ: 'I will boast all the more gladly about my weaknesses, so that Christ's power may rest on me' (v9). These words are breathtaking. Boast about weaknesses? Bring the power of Christ? In Paul's letters to the Corinthians, we will see how a passion for Christ transforms our perspective in *any* situation. The greatest burden on Paul's soul was the advance of the gospel. This was a man with the cross on his heart and whose life was laid out before his crucified Lord.

I pray that as we study his letters, we may echo Paul's words and live with renewed passion for Christ and for the gospel, and be willing, if necessary, to suffer for His sake and to turn that very suffering to His glory.

Sharing in the sufferings of Christ

'we share abundantly in the sufferings of Christ' (2 Cor. 1:5)

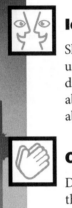

Icebreaker

Share about a time in your life when someone has totally and unexpectedly shown you loving compassion or comfort. How did you feel as the recipient of such an act? Alternatively, share about a loving incident of such that you have seen or heard about that particularly moved you.

Opening Prayer

Dear Father, we thank You for all the compassion and comfort that You have given to us across the years; for the strength and grace given to us in times of suffering. Please help us now to understand more fully the depth of suffering that Jesus bore to free us from our sins, and help us to grasp more fully what it means for us to share in His sufferings and to convey His comfort. Amen.

Setting the Scene

One of Paul's aims in writing to the Corinthians for the second time is to deal with a situation where false apostles have twisted the true gospel. He chides the church later for being easy prey to the preaching of a false Jesus, a different spirit and a different gospel (2 Cor. 11:4). Wrong teaching brings, of course, wrong outcomes, such as being morally weak, failing in giving (chapters 8 and 9) and especially in their views on suffering. They have the marks of what we call these days 'the prosperity gospel'. So anxious is he to correct their wrong thinking on suffering that Paul plunges straight in after the initial greetings.

The church in Corinth had revelled in experiencing prophecies, tongues and other spiritual gifts, and suffering was seen as something that shouldn't happen to Christians. Paul, however, wants them to see how it can be the very seed-bed of witness and can be used in the service of Christ and in testimony to grace and divine comfort. No doubt all of us can apply the teaching here to situations in which we have been involved personally or with others.

Bible Readings

2 Corinthians 1:3–11

'Praise be to the God and Father of our Lord Jesus
Christ, the Father of compassion and the God of
all comfort, who comforts us in all our troubles, so
that we can comfort those in any trouble with the
comfort we ourselves receive from God. For just as
we share abundantly in the sufferings of Christ, so
also our comfort abounds through Christ. If we are
distressed, it is for your comfort and salvation; if we
are comforted, it is for your comfort, which produces
in you patient endurance of the same sufferings we
suffer. And our hope for you is firm, because we know
that just as you share in our sufferings, so also you
share in our comfort.

We do not want you to be uninformed, brothers and
sisters, about the troubles we experienced in the province
of Asia. We were under great pressure, far beyond
our ability to endure, so that we despaired of life itself.
Indeed, we felt we had received the sentence of death. But
this happened that we might not rely on ourselves but on
God, who raises the dead. He has delivered us from such
a deadly peril, and he will deliver us again. On him we
have set our hope that he will continue to deliver us, as
you help us by your prayers. Then many will give thanks
on our behalf for the gracious favour granted us in
answer to the prayers of many.'

2 Corinthians 6:3–8

'We put no stumbling-block in anyone's path, so that
our ministry will not be discredited. Rather, as servants
of God we commend ourselves in every way: in great
endurance; in troubles, hardships and distresses; in
beatings, imprisonments and riots; in hard work, sleepless
nights and hunger; in purity, understanding, patience
and kindness; in the Holy Spirit and in sincere love; in
truthful speech and in the power of God; with weapons

of righteousness in the right hand and in the left; through glory and dishonour, bad report and good report'

1 Peter 4:13–14,16,19
'But rejoice inasmuch as you participate in the sufferings of Christ, so that you may be overjoyed when his glory is revealed. If you are insulted because of the name of Christ, you are blessed, for the Spirit of glory and of God rests on you… However, if you suffer as a Christian, do not be ashamed, but praise God that you bear that name… those who suffer according to God's will should commit themselves to their faithful Creator and continue to do good.'

Session Focus

The start of Paul's letter is unexpected. Instead of focusing on actual suffering, he lifts their whole perspective to God as Father. He has found the experiences of suffering to be the arena of great comfort; he has known God as the 'Father of compassion' (2 Cor. 1:3) and as the one who does not just comfort just occasionally but who does so 'in all our troubles' (v4). The word translated 'troubles' is better translated as 'pressures', which we can easily relate to in our pressured society. Reading Paul's list in chapter six of all that he suffered reminds us that he experienced more pressure than most of us. His response, however, is not one of complaining or believing there must be something wrong with his spiritual life that is causing this pressure, but one of testimony and praise for the comfort and compassionate actions of the Father. Sometimes, it seems we can be so consumed with our suffering that we are blind to the touches of God's love and compassion. Paul was not. Sensing God's presence in bleak times was, for him, as it can be to us, a great encouragement.

The Greek word for 'comfort' is *paraklesis*, and the Holy Spirit is referred to as the Paraclete, meaning 'called alongside', which reminds us that He is with us in the darkest of situations. The first three verses of Psalm 23 refer to the

Lord in the third person: 'He makes me like down in green pastures' (v2). But in the valley of the shadow of death (v4), it is no longer 'He' or 'the Lord', but 'You', showing the deeper closeness of God in the midst of suffering. Over the years, I have known many faithful churchgoers who have been thrown onto God in a new way when facing suffering or bereavement, and have come to know Him personally for the first time or more deeply than ever before. The God of compassion has touched them and brought them near to Him.

Then there is another surprise. Not only does Paul push our thinking upward, he now pushes it outwards by reminding us to comfort others in the same way (2 Cor. 1:4). Like a railway line, he does not see himself simply as the final destination for God's comfort but more as a great junction through which the same comfort can be shared with others.

In verse 5, he gives this perfect balance for the believer: 'For just as we share abundantly in the sufferings of Christ, so also our comfort abounds through Christ.' Note the word 'abounds' – God's comfort is plentiful! In their understandable desperation to be healed, men and women may miss out on the comfort, peace, compassion and surrounding love of God. I recall one clergyman, who had terminal cancer, dismissing me when I went to see him in hospital. He did not need comfort, he said, because he was going to be healed. He would shout at God in the ward, and only in his last two days did he let go and enter into peace and comfort.

Some people will identify with the moment when Paul thought he had 'received the sentence of death' (v9), when it is beyond one's ability to endure, when there seems to be no answer to an impossible situation. But so often in those situations, when we are thrown entirely onto God, the impossible becomes the possible; there is an unexpected intervention that we cannot explain from the God 'who raises the dead' (v9). Paul gratefully acknowledges their prayers for him during 'such a deadly peril' (v10). When a friend or fellow believer is going through such a difficult trial that they are not even able to pray, let's take the strain and carry them in earnest prayer.

Discussion Starters

1. 'Compassion' means 'suffering with', so what does 'Father of compassion' (2 Cor. 1:3) mean for you? Have you ever praised God in those terms? Share with your group special experiences of God's compassion and comfort abounding in your life, resulting in a deeper knowledge of His love.

_____
_____
_____
_____

2. According to Paul, one result of suffering is that we can comfort others with the same comfort that we have received (vv4–6). Discuss what this might mean or has meant in your experience. What sort of comforting is helpful – and what is unhelpful?

_____
_____
_____
_____

3. Paul speaks of sharing the sufferings of Christ. What do you think this means in our Christian lives and devotion to our Lord? Look at Paul's list (2 Cor. 6:4–5) and think of when Jesus experienced similar (and additional) sufferings. What response does this comparison evoke in you?

_____
_____
_____
_____

4. How do you respond to the verses in 1 Peter 4? Are we able to stand up for Christ when we know it will bring negative reaction, even suffering? Share if you have experienced this.

    _____

    _____

    _____

    _____

5. Read 2 Corinthians 6:6–8 (up to 'good report') and reflect on Paul's Christlike attitude and commitment when facing suffering. What stands out for you as you read these verses?

    _____

    _____

    _____

    _____

6. How would you comfort a distraught believer who has been told their loved one would not have died if they had had more faith or confessed hidden sins? How would you show compassion to someone who still believes in God but not in a God of love, following the death of their child in a car accident?

    _____

    _____

    _____

    _____

7. In 2 Corinthians 1:11, Paul writes that he has been helped through a desperate situation by the Corinthians' prayers. Do you belong to an emergency prayer chain? Share any testimonies you have of this.

    _____

    _____

    _____

    _____

Final Thoughts

In Romans 5:1–5, Paul writes about being justified by faith, having peace with God, access into His grace and hope of the glory of God, but he then suddenly blows our minds by stating, 'Not only so, but we also glory in our sufferings' (v3). Why? How? Not because of the sufferings themselves but what going through them can do for us: 'because we know that suffering produces perseverance; perseverance, character; and character, hope. And hope does not put us to shame, because God's love has been poured into our hearts through the Holy Spirit, who has been given to us' (vv3–4). Isn't that thrilling? We are not to look down at the suffering but up at the Lord in order to grow in usefulness for Him and into the deepening experience of His love.

Closing Prayer

Praise be to You, the God and Father of our Lord Jesus Christ, the Father of compassion and the God of all comfort, who comforts us in all our troubles, so that we can comfort those in any trouble with the comfort we receive from You (2 Cor. 1:3–4). May we do so, in Your name. Amen.

Further Reflection

'Christ does not explain suffering or explain it away – but He changes everything. He would turn the world's supreme tragedy into the world's supreme testimony – and He did!' – Ernest Stanley Jones.

Think about the way Jesus turned His suffering and death tragedy into the greatest victory for the world. Would you be able to turn your own difficult times into an opportunity to share with others your continuing dependence on your loving God?

For further reading, I recommend: E. Stanley Jones, *Christ and Human Suffering* (London: Hodder and Stoughton, 1933).

Seeking love in the Church of Christ

'for I wrote to you... to let you know the depth of my love for you.' (2 Cor. 1:4)

Icebreaker

In a similar way to the TV panel show *Would I lie to you?*, ask members of the group to share an event (real or imagined) that has supposedly happened to them. Other members are to decide whether the event was true or a lie.

Opening Prayer

Lord, we are conscious of how much You want Your church to be marked by love and holiness. Help us now, we pray, to see this need more clearly, and to learn how You want us to deal with any divisions and lack of love in our lives. For Your name's sake. Amen.

Setting the Scene

When Jesus said, 'love each other as I have loved you' (John 15:12), it was not a hopeful suggestion – it was a command. The Corinthians seemed to be failing in this: they did not love one another. Back in 1 Corinthians 1:10, Paul had appealed to them 'in the name of our Lord Jesus Christ, that all of you agree with one another in what you say and that there be no divisions among you'. Later he criticised their lack of love at the Communion gatherings because some brought their own food and did not share it: 'do you despise the church of God by humiliating those who have nothing?' (1 Cor. 11:22). He capped this by writing: 'If I speak in the tongues of men or of angels, but do not have love, I am only a resounding gong or a clanging cymbal' (1 Cor. 13:1). Paul longs for them to have love that matches their calling as God's 'holy people' (1 Cor. 1:2 and 2 Cor. 1:1).

In 2 Corinthians 1:12–2:11, Paul has to deal with the false rumour about himself, with their loveless accusations against him of supposed inconsistency. He also has to urge them to balance the heavy judgment they had imposed on the immoral person by instead showing love and mercy (2 Cor. 2:5–8).

Bible Readings

2 Corinthians 1:12,16–20

'we have conducted ourselves in the world, and especially in our relations with you, with integrity and godly sincerity… I wanted to visit you… Was I fickle when I intended to do this? Or do I make my plans in a worldly manner so that in the same breath I say both "Yes, yes" and "No, no"? But as surely as God is faithful, our message to you is not "Yes" and "No". For the Son of God, Jesus Christ… was not "Yes" and "No", but in him it has always been "Yes". For no matter how many promises God has made, they are "Yes" in Christ. And so through him the "Amen" is spoken by us to the glory of God.'

2 Corinthians 1:21–22

'Now it is God who makes both us and you stand firm in Christ. He anointed us, set his seal of ownership on us, and put his Spirit in our hearts as a deposit, guaranteeing what is to come.'

2 Corinthians 1:23; 2:4

'I call God as my witness – and I stake my life on it – that it was in order to spare you that I did not return to Corinth… For I wrote to you out of great distress and anguish of heart and with many tears, not to grieve you but to let you know the depth of my love for you.'

2 Corinthians 2:5–8,10–11

'If anyone has caused grief, he has not so much grieved me as he has grieved all of you to some extent - not to put it too severely. The punishment inflicted on him by the majority is sufficient. Now instead, you ought to forgive and comfort him, so that he will not be overwhelmed by excessive sorrow. I urge you, therefore, to reaffirm your love for him… Anyone you forgive, I also forgive. And what I have forgiven – if there was anything to forgive – I have forgiven in the sight of Christ for your

sake, in order that Satan might not outwit us. For we are not unaware of his schemes.'

Ephesians 5:25–27
'Christ loved the church and gave himself up for her to make her holy, cleansing her by the washing with water through the word, and to present her to himself as a radiant church, without stain or wrinkle or any other blemish, but holy and blameless.'

Session Focus

The way the false teachers had poisoned the minds of the Corinthians about Paul's suffering would have created an atmosphere in which they would have believed any false rumour about him without checking. We can easily do the same thing once we have heard a negative rumour or report about someone. You may, like me, have suffered from totally false assumptions and accusations, even from fellow Christians. This isn't the mark of a holy people. Yet we should not be surprised as we remember the narratives of Christ's Passion and the false accusations, condemnations and suffering He endured for us – we share His sufferings.

That Paul has to defend himself is sad to read; that the Corinthians accused him of lacking in integrity takes one's breath away. He was a man of such utter integrity. These days integrity is increasingly the valued mark of Christians in business and in all walks of life. The expectation is that we are true to our word without a hidden agenda. But is our word to be totally trusted?

We all have our own points of view and differing opinions, but often these need to be challenged. In 2 Corinthians 1:21, Paul goes to the root of what unites him and the Corinthians: God has anointed them both. They are both established in Christ, both sealed by the Spirit, both guaranteed for what is to come (v22).

Carefully dealing with the person who has caused grief is a delicate balance between judgment and mercy, condemnation and forgiveness. It seems as if the Corinthian church members had come down hard on a person who was in danger of suffering from 'excessive sorrow' (2 Cor. 2:7). They are not only urged to forgive but to reaffirm their love for him. This is the root of their problem – can they love? Despite Paul's encouragement to love one another in his first letter (1 Cor. 13:1–13), the Corinthians are still finding it hard to put it into practice.

It was love that made Paul cancel his possible visit because he did not want to hurt them (2 Cor. 2:1). His great distress and anguish of heart (v4) is because of his deep love for them. In spite of their denigration of him, their false accusations and assumptions, he still loves them deeply. What a lesson!

Paul then gives a sharp reminder that lack of forgiveness and poor judgment can open the way for differences to escalate into very bitter division, which, in turn, can become strident condemnation, splitting the church and leaving many wounded. How Satan must want that. Once, I was preaching at a church that was facing a colossal challenge which had divided the congregation. When I came to prepare my sermon, I had the unusual experience of knowing precisely what was required of me by God; He was obviously planning what was to happen. It was a privilege to be there that night as the Spirit moved in the congregation, and, at the end, people around the church moved towards one another to seek forgiveness and to renew their love for one another. Such love was as the Lord commanded in John 15:12: 'love each other as I have loved you'. Divisions became secondary; love took priority. The church came back on track with God.

The verses in Ephesians 5 and 2 Corinthians 2:1–4 both underline Paul's passion for the Church. It is the passion of Christ Himself. Our Saviour loves the Church – I repeat, He loves the Church – but He wants it to be a radiant Church: holy, blameless, without blemish or spot. The thought of how some Christians have besmirched the Church today will surely make us want to pray with passion for the Church, locally and worldwide, to glorify Christ and to be the fountain-place of God's love. A passion of love for Christ involves a passion of love for His Church!

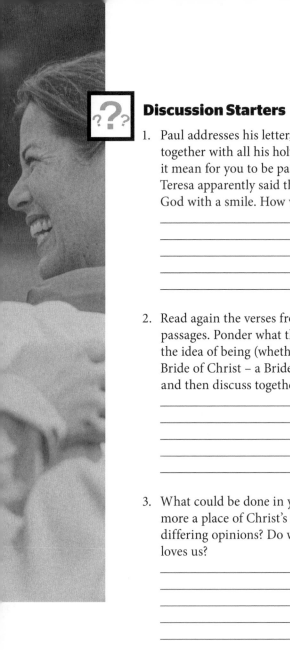

Discussion Starters

1. Paul addresses his letter, 'To the church of God in Corinth, together with all his holy people' (2 Cor. 1:1). What does it mean for you to be part of God's 'holy people'? Mother Teresa apparently said that holiness is doing the will of God with a smile. How would you define holiness?

   _____

   _____

   _____

   _____

   _____

2. Read again the verses from Ephesians 5 in the Bible passages. Ponder what this means in your life, especially the idea of being (whether man or woman) part of the Bride of Christ – a Bride being prepared by the Bridegroom, and then discuss together.

   _____

   _____

   _____

   _____

   _____

3. What could be done in your local church to make it even more a place of Christ's love? Does love take priority over differing opinions? Do we love one another as Christ loves us?

   _____

   _____

   _____

   _____

   _____

4. How do we expose false rumours and quick denigration of others? Do we check the facts instead of listening to gossip? How do we seek to support those falsely attacked? Paul reminds us that 'Love does not delight in evil but rejoices with the truth. It always protects' (1 Cor. 13:6–7).

_____

_____

_____

_____

_____

5. Becoming so divided and judgmental that we fail to forgive and lovingly restore is Satan's way of outwitting the Church. Share any experiences of being in a fractured church group and how relationships were restored, if at all.

_____

_____

_____

_____

_____

6. Share what it means to you that you are anointed, sealed, guaranteed for what is to come and have the Spirit in your heart (2 Cor. 1:21–22).

_____

_____

_____

_____

_____

Final Thoughts

Paul's passion and concern for the Church of Christ influenced what he wrote. He did not ignore serious issues. He tackled the situation and, if appropriate, we must lovingly do the same. The letters to the Corinthians had been taken by hand. Without today's instant communications, it would have been weeks, perhaps months, before Paul knew how they had reacted. He wrote of having 'conflicts on the outside, fears within' (2 Cor. 7:5).* But Paul's faithful missionary companion, Titus, brought him some comforting news – 'godly sorrow' that had caused the Corinthians to repent. Paul was overjoyed because he knew that true repentance 'leads to salvation and leaves no regret, but worldly sorrow brings death' (v10). Isn't it wonderful that we can receive forgiveness, restoration and peace when we truly repent?

May we be stirred to pray earnestly for Christ's Church, with the passion for Christ that burns in our hearts. Let us pray for love to overflow in and from our churches, and in and from our lives, to the glory of our beloved Saviour.

Closing Prayer

Lord Jesus, who wept over Jerusalem on the road to Your death, please forgive us for what must grieve You in Your Church in this day. Help us to be holy, to be faithful, to be peacemakers, and to stand unswervingly for Your truth, Your will and way and Your saving gospel, that we may glorify Your name in Your Church and in our lives. Amen.

Further Reflection

Ask someone to read Ephesians 3:14–21, and resolve to pray for one another and for others in your church to be 'filled to the measure of all the fullness of God' (v19) for 'glory in the church and in Christ Jesus' (v20).

*This verse inspired some of the words in the hymn, *Just as I am, without one plea*, by Charlotte Elliott:. 'Just as I am, though tossed about with many a conflict, many a doubt, fightings and fears within, without, O Lamb of God, I come, I come.'

Spreading the aroma of Christ

'spread the aroma of the knowledge of him everywhere.' (2 Cor. 2:14)

Icebreaker

Share with the group some of your favourite aromas
(eg roasting coffee, sea air, food, perfume) and say what
associations these aromas have for you (eg a special place or
event).

Opening Prayer

Lord, as we study today's passages from Your Word, we pray
that the Holy Spirit will open them to us and bring results in
our lives for You. We thank You for all those who helped us
come to faith and who have encouraged us to follow Christ.
May we be faithful messengers and encouragers by our words
and lives. Amen.

Setting the Scene

Most of us know what it is like to have something concerning
us that we think about through the day and often through the
night. It is worse if we cannot do anything about the problem.
All Paul can do regarding the problems in Corinth is to write
a letter and send Titus with it. He then journeys in the same
direction, in the hope of meeting Titus on his return trip.
In Troas, he doesn't meet Titus but the Lord 'opened a door'
(2 Cor. 2:12). Paul loved that term and used it several times.
Clearly, there was encouragement. The gospel was welcomed,
he was able to open his heart and speak of Jesus and there was
fruit. But he is restless and carries on his journey.

Paul's tone then changes; there is an amazing outburst of
confidence, joy and a renewed commitment to his task. It is
a lesson to us that even when unsettled about some challenge
in our lives, we can turn our eyes towards our Lord, we can
seek His power and grace and rest on the fact that whatever
happens we cannot be separated from Him. This does not
necessarily mean the unease disappears but it is outmatched
by the lordship of Christ.

Bible Readings

2 Corinthians 2:12–17

'Now when I went to Troas to preach the gospel of Christ and found that the Lord had opened a door for me, I still had no peace of mind, because I did not find my brother Titus there. So I said goodbye to them and went on to Macedonia.

But thanks be to God, who always leads us as captives in Christ's triumphal procession and uses us to spread the aroma of the knowledge of him everywhere. For we are to God the pleasing aroma of Christ among those who are being saved and those who are perishing. To the one we are an aroma that brings death; to the other an aroma that brings life. And who is equal to such a task? Unlike so many, we do not peddle the word of God for profit. On the contrary, in Christ we speak before God with sincerity, as those sent from God.'

2 Corinthians 3:1–6

'Are we beginning to commend ourselves again? Or do we need, like some people, letters of recommendation to you or from you? You yourselves are our letter, written on our hearts, known and read by everyone. You show that you are a letter from Christ, the result of our ministry, written not with ink but with the Spirit of the living God, not on tablets of stone but on tablets of human hearts.

Such confidence we have through Christ before God. Not that we are competent in ourselves to claim anything for ourselves, but our competence comes from God. He has made us competent as ministers of a new covenant – not of the letter but of the Spirit; for the letter kills, but the Spirit gives life.'

Colossians 2:13–15

'When you were dead in your sins and in the uncircumcision of your flesh, God made you alive with Christ. He forgave us all our sins, having cancelled the

charge of our legal indebtedness, which stood against us
and condemned us; he has taken it away, nailing it to the
cross. And having disarmed the powers and authorities,
he made a public spectacle of them, triumphing over
them by the cross.'

1 Corinthians 15:54–57
'…"Death has been swallowed up in victory." "Where,
O death, is your victory? Where, O death, is your sting?"
The sting of death is sin, and the power of sin is the law.
But thanks be to God! He gives us the victory through
our Lord Jesus Christ.'

Romans 8:35,37
'Who shall separate us from the love of Christ? Shall
trouble or hardship or persecution or famine or
nakedness or danger or sword?... No, in all these things
we are more than conquerors through him who loved us.'

Session Focus

Paul lifts his eyes off his restlessness, onto the glorious
certainties of being Christ's. He uses the picture of a victorious
Roman general in a triumphant procession and he elevates
the idea to Christ leading us in His victory over sin and death.
The priests would have been spreading incense all the way, the
aroma filling the air, and its scent would be on everyone – the
conquered captives as well as the joyful army. Paul says that
'God… leads us as captives' (2 Cor. 2:14, the Greek word for
'captive' means 'triumphed over'), which might seem negative
but it means that we are trophies of grace, people in whom
Satan's hold has been broken, who have been released from
slavery to death and are now the thrilled followers of the one
who achieved that triumph. We might say we are not captives
but captivated!

Paul now takes the picture further. We are the actual aroma
filling the air, the 'aroma of Christ' (v15), 'the aroma of the
knowledge of him everywhere' (v14). Our aroma-filled lives are

pleasing to God. It is an awesome responsibility and a deeply moving truth that when we are walking with Christ and being indwelt by the Spirit, we are giving off the scent of Christ.

This 'aroma' of our lives can have different effects on people. In the Roman procession metaphor, the same incense smell would have been a delight to the followers of the general but would have meant defeat and death to the conquered armies.

Increasingly today, there are polar opposite reactions to Christians. Wherever we are – our neighbourhood, workplace, college, or on holiday – we soon sense the aroma of Christ in others and are drawn into fellowship with them. Those against Christ, however, also sense the aroma of Christ in us and often avoid us or even oppose us.

The concept of Christ's triumph is spelt out in Colossians (2:13–15). It is sometimes referred to as the 'Christus Victor' picture of the cross. The triumph over us is that of salvation, of forgiveness and being made alive in Christ. The conquest of the cross is of the 'powers and authorities' (v15) that were ranged against our Lord.

This strengthens Paul's resolve to be effective as a witness. He despises the 'peddlers' of the Word (peddlers were known as those who could sell anything effectively because of their 'gift of the gab'). The false apostles were peddlers. For Paul, preaching and speaking had to be with total integrity and sincerity. Most of all, and I regularly examine my own heart about this, we are to 'speak before God with sincerity, as those sent from God' (2 Cor. 2:17). When preparing sermons (or writing Bible study notes), I have learnt not to focus on how many people might be listening (or reading) but to focus on doing my very best for my Lord.

I once was taking a group of ordinands (trainee vicars) from a training conference in the Peak District to an inner-city parish in Manchester, to do house-to-house visiting. It was peaceful enough as our journey began but gradually, as we entered Manchester, some of the group became nervous about the task ahead. One young man, desperately turning the pages of his Bible, cried: 'Where does it say, "who is equal to such a task?"' I went and sat with him and then turned his attention

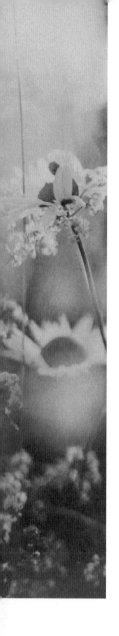

to: 'Such confidence we have through Christ before God. Not that we are competent in ourselves to claim anything for ourselves, but our competence comes from God' (2 Cor. 3:4–5).

It is amazing how many people try to dismiss thoughts of an afterlife by saying there is nothing after death, but underneath are actually avoiding the real issue. Some years ago, Michael Parkinson was interviewing Cliff Richard on TV and challenged him to consider the idea of there being no life after death. Cliff paused, looked 'Parky' in the eye, and challenged him to consider the idea of there indeed being life after death. Parkinson went white. Cliff, and all of us who know Christ as Saviour, live in the triumph of Christ and thus know the confidence of resurrection to eternal life. I think sometimes we almost take it for granted, but what a victorious state to be in. This hope, says Hebrews 6:19 is an 'anchor for the soul, firm and secure.'

As we walk in God's triumphal procession, let us join with Paul in declaring: 'thanks be to God! He gives us the victory through our Lord Jesus Christ' (1 Cor. 15:57).

Discussion Starters

1. Share occasions when you have been drawn to certain people, only to discover that they are followers of Christ too. Discuss what it means to be 'the pleasing aroma of Christ' (2 Cor. 2:15).

_____

_____

_____

_____

2. Share occasions or circumstances when your presence, or the presence of another, as a Christian has not been welcome. How did you respond?

_____

_____

_____

_____

3. How strengthened and encouraged are you by Colossians 2:13–15? Discuss the difference between living in the triumph of Christ and being triumphalist – for yourself and for churches.

_____

_____

_____

_____

4. Imagine a Christian friend is not certain about their resurrection to eternal life. How would you try to help her/him? What scriptures might be helpful?

_____

_____

_____

_____

5. Paul overcomes his disappointments by laying a strong hold on what it means to be Christ's. If appropriate, share occasions when you have done the same when dealing with disappointment. How does knowing that 'we are more than conquerors through him' (Rom. 8:37) also help?

_____
_____
_____
_____

6. If you speak or preach for Christ, how do you avoid being a 'peddler' of God's Word, and how might you challenge any who devalue God's Word by insincerity?

_____
_____
_____
_____

7. Look at 2 Corinthians 3:2–3. How does this ring true in your experience?

_____
_____
_____
_____

Final Thoughts

In our own strength, we are not able to convert anyone. Forced conversions are false conversions, which are often the result of human pressure, cults and the like. True conversions are the work of the Holy Spirit, who is the guardian of the convert (2 Cor. 3:1–3,6). Paul came to Corinth, an immoral place, not with eloquence or human wisdom, but to preach 'Jesus Christ and him crucified' (1 Cor. 2:2). He did so 'in weakness with great fear and trembling… but with a demonstration of the Spirit's power' (vv3,4). The result was that God the Holy Spirit worked and brought the most unlikely people to Christ (1 Cor. 6:9–11). The Spirit wrote the letter; Paul delivered it. May we all be faithful postmen and postwomen for Christ.

Closing Prayer

Lord Jesus, we thank You so much for Your saving Word and we thank You, Holy Spirit, for the way You write that Word on people's hearts. Thank You for writing it on our hearts. Help us to be effective and faithful deliverers of the letter to others. Amen.

Further Reflection

Walking day by day in the triumph of Christ, being His aroma wherever we are and being deliverers of the gospel to others – that is a lot to reflect and act on but we are able to do so: 'Not that we are competent in ourselves… but our competence comes from God' (2 Cor. 3:5).

Shining with the light of Christ

'the light of the gospel that displays the glory of Christ' (2 Cor. 4:4)

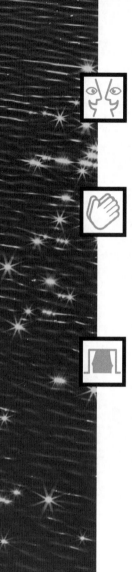

Icebreaker

Share experiences of suddenly being dazzled by bright light, such as driving into a low-setting sun. Now imagine Paul on the Damascus road, dazzled by God's glory. What do you think was happening to him?

Opening Prayer

Beloved Lord, You who showed Your divine glory on earth, please help us now as we think about the wonder of Your glory in today's readings. Touch our hearts with Your glory and prepare us for heaven where one day we will cry, 'To him who sits on the throne and to the Lamb be praise and honour and glory and power, for ever and ever!' (Rev. 5:13). Amen.

Setting the Scene

After teaching for years in Corinth and seeing many come out of darkness into the light of Christ, Paul must have been disheartened when he learnt that false teachers were persuading people to go back to the old covenant of Moses with its rules and promises. The Ten Commandments came with glory but that glory faded, showing the temporary nature of the old covenant.

Through Christ's death and resurrection, a new permanent covenant had been established – a personal covenant with God (Jer. 31:31–34). Paul clearly saw that this was by faith and grace, and not by law; that it only came through the light of the gospel and would be with unfading glory for ever. He longs for them to wake up, to turn back to Christ, the light of the world, and to experience the illumination, the radical transformation, the joy and assurance of living in His light.

Bible Readings

2 Corinthians 3:7–18

'Now if the ministry that brought death, which was engraved in letters of stone, came with glory, so that the Israelites could not look steadily at the face of Moses because of its glory, transitory though it was, will not the ministry of the Spirit be even more glorious? If the ministry that brought condemnation was glorious, how much more glorious is the ministry that brings righteousness! For what was glorious has no glory now in comparison with the surpassing glory. And if what was transitory came with glory, how much greater is the glory of that which lasts!'

Therefore, since we have such a hope, we are very bold. We are not like Moses, who would put a veil over his face to prevent the Israelites from seeing the end of what was passing away. But their minds were made dull, for to this day the same veil remains when the old covenant is read. It has not been removed, because only in Christ is it taken away. Even to this day when Moses is read, a veil covers their hearts. But whenever anyone turns to the Lord, the veil is taken away. Now the Lord is the Spirit, and where the Spirit of the Lord is, there is freedom. And we all, who with unveiled faces contemplate the Lord's glory, are being transformed into his image with ever-increasing glory, which comes from the Lord, who is the Spirit.'

2 Corinthians 4:1–6

'Therefore, since through God's mercy we have this ministry, we do not lose heart. Rather, we have renounced secret and shameful ways; we do not use deception, nor do we distort the word of God. On the contrary, by setting forth the truth plainly we commend ourselves to everyone's conscience in the sight of God. And even if our gospel is veiled, it is veiled to those who are perishing. The god of this age has blinded the minds of unbelievers, so that they cannot see the light of the gospel that displays the glory of Christ, who is the image of God. For what

we preach is not ourselves, but Jesus Christ as Lord, and ourselves as your servants for Jesus' sake. For God, who said, "Let light shine out of darkness," made his light shine in our hearts to give us the light of the knowledge of God's glory displayed in the face of Christ.'

Session Focus

The tragedy in the first part of today's reading is the sheer blindness that stops people seeing the truth of the liberating gospel. Paul is referring to his hearers and to Israelites when he says that 'a veil covers their hearts' (2 Cor. 3:15), but maybe you can think of neighbours, work colleagues or others whom you have tried to share your faith with, only to be constantly met with spiritually-blinded eyes. Why? There is nothing wrong with the gospel but the 'god of this age has blinded the minds of unbelievers' (2 Cor. 4:4). We know it all started back in Genesis 3:1, when Satan cast doubt: 'Did God really say...?' Paul refers to Satan as 'the ruler of the kingdom of the air, the spirit who is at work in those who are disobedient' (Eph. 2:2).

So first let us pause and realise afresh that we are in a battle when we are seeking to witness to others. Truth is vital but so is prayer. Perhaps that is why Jesus sent the disciples out two by two in Luke 10 – one to speak, one to pray. The battle requires serious prayer, not mere mentions; it requires taking time for extended prayer for relatives or contacts who are blind to the gospel. The Corinthians would certainly have been on Paul's heart (and prayer list) night and day.

Let us go back to the thrilling verse: 'whenever anyone turns to the Lord, the veil is taken away' (2 Cor. 3:16). There is no greater joy than seeing the veil fall away and seeing someone enter into the joy of faith in Christ. After praying and sharing the good news, it is always a moment of sheer wonder, for me, when someone opens up to God and is immediately different. Where once there was resistance and darkness, light now begins to shine in their eyes as well as their souls. It is the Holy Spirit, says Paul. He gives freedom!

Some years ago, my wife Myrtle and I went to the Solomon

Islands to launch the bond between the Province of Melanesia and our Diocese of Chester. At a gathering in one of the communities, the ladies sang while the men, dressed in war dress and war paint, danced a Christianised war dance! Then an elderly man came up to me and said, 'When you go back to England, tell them we can never thank them enough for bringing us Jesus and setting us free.' He then presented me with a dagger and added, 'If they hadn't, you would have been killed, as we were a cannibalistic race.' I was deeply moved. Freedom. What it meant to them! What does it mean to us?

As we gaze on the Lord's glory, Paul says that 'we are being transformed into his image with ever-increasing glory, which comes from the Lord, who is the Spirit' (2 Cor. 3:18). Isn't that absolutely wonderful? I once belonged to a 'Wesley Club' of male singers and we used to thunder out the words: 'From glory to glory he leads me on, from grace to grace every day.' Transformation will be gradual, but it should show. When Christians do not gaze, they do not change to be more like Christ, and that sadly shows too.

Truth was a vital part of Paul's armour and he lets the Corinthians have truth again and again (2 Cor. 4:1–6). The false teachers may think they have made difficulties for him but he insists 'we do not lose heart'. Why? Because his ministry is 'through God's mercy' (v1) – on him, and in the new covenant in Christ. Paul blasts the false apostles out of the water. He rejects their secret and shameful ways, their deception and distortion of the Word of God. To pronounce such a condemnation takes knowledge, courage and confidence in the gospel of Christ.

Then comes that stimulating sentence: 'by setting forth the truth plainly we commend ourselves to everyone's conscience in the sight of God' (4:2). Paul certainly did speak the truth, just like the Lord Jesus. What a model for us to follow. As I wrote earlier, *we* cannot convert people but we can speak the truth plainly (or learn how to do so). It is then over to the hearer to hear, and the Holy Spirit to move. May we say with Paul: 'what we preach is not ourselves, but Jesus Christ as Lord, and ourselves as your servants for Jesus' sake' (4:5).

Discussion Starters

1. As people of the new covenant, what is our attitude to the old covenant? Is it still of value to us? What does the new covenant mean to us? And what do the words: 'This cup is the new covenant in my blood' (Luke 22:20) mean to us?

   _____

   _____

   _____

   _____

   _____

2. Can any of the group relate to going through a time of resisting God? What contributed to their blindness and what triggered their turning to Christ?

   _____

   _____

   _____

   _____

   _____

3. Discuss how we 'contemplate the Lord's glory... which comes from the Lord, who is the Spirit' (2 Cor. 3:18). The Greek word for 'contemplate' can also mean 'reflect', as the moon reflects the sun rather than having its own light. How do we similarly reflect Christ's glory?

   _____

   _____

   _____

   _____

   _____

4. Are you aware of any teachings that are a distortion of
    the Word of God? Have any of the group been able to find
    materials or attend courses that can help challenge such
    teaching?

    _____

    _____

    _____

    _____

    _____

5. Sharing biblical truths plainly is always a challenge. What
    seems to be the most effective way of doing this? Discuss
    what are some of the non-negotiable gospel truths.

    _____

    _____

    _____

    _____

    _____

6. The angels sang 'Glory to God in the highest' (Luke 2:14) at
    the birth of Jesus. Think together of as many ways as you
    can of giving glory to God.

    _____

    _____

    _____

    _____

    _____

7. What does 2 Corinthians 4:6 mean for you? How can we
    ensure that we are letting 'his light shine in our hearts'?

    _____

    _____

    _____

    _____

    _____

Final Thoughts

As a teenager, I was fortunate to be given the chance to attend the Royal Albert Hall for a performance of Haydn's *Creation*. The smog from outside seeped into the hall, making the atmosphere seem somewhat ethereal. I did not know the classical piece so was taken by complete surprise when it came to: 'Let there be light. And there was... LIGHT.' That last word was thunderously loud, with full orchestra playing, the enormous choir singing plus the great organ. But that shock was nothing compared with discovering and experiencing the truth that the same God who brought light to the whole universe out of darkness had actually brought light to me in my spiritual darkness – and, I trust, to you. It is God's light that shows us the truth, opens up the Bible to become a living Word, and gives us the knowledge of God's glory in the face of Christ. It is just too wonderful. When I remember God's saving grace, I am always – even right now – overcome with tears of wonder, thanksgiving, worship and adoration.

Closing Devotion

Graham Kendrick's well-known song *Shine, Jesus, Shine* superbly encapsulates and expresses what we have been studying today. I suggest that instead of singing it, you join together in praying it.

Further Reflection

I hope that after this study, the word 'glory' will leap out at you in prayers, readings, in the Gloria Excelsis and in hymns such as *To God be the glory, Thine be the glory* and, especially at Easter, *Glory be to Jesus*.

Showing the life of Jesus in our mortal bodies

'his life may also be revealed in our mortal body' (2 Cor. 4:11)

Icebreaker

If any members of the group have a disability or experience of long-term illness or injury (and feel comfortable to share), ask whether they have been able to turn this into something positive.

Opening Prayer

Lord, as we live in this fallen world, we pray for grace to cope with the events in life that hurt us and we also pray for fellow Christians around the world who are suffering. Help us and them to draw more fully on the indwelling power of the Spirit, to Your glory. Amen.

Setting the Scene

Now we are the focus. What a shock! We have just been lifted up to glory and told of that glory in us. Then comes the 'But' (2 Cor. 4:7). We are fragile humans, like jars of clay; if you drop us, we crack or break. Our bodies, though wonderfully made, are mortal. The contrast between the glory in us and our fragile state is a powerful testimony.

My wife, Myrtle, was a watercolour painter. Every few months we went to the framers and spent time choosing a frame that would best display the latest painting to its full glory. Paul says that when we are 'perplexed, but not in despair… the life of Jesus may also be revealed in our body' (2 Cor. 4:8–10). Suffering is like a frame, which draws the eye to a person's faith. When Christians seem to have everything and speak of their faith, people seldom give them much thought. But if a Christian is suffering – whether it be physically, emotionally or financially – and they are radiating the glory of Christ in their lives, then the outsider has to stop and take notice.

Bible Readings

2 Corinthians 4:7–18

'But we have this treasure in jars of clay to show that
this all-surpassing power is from God and not from
us. We are hard pressed on every side, *but* not crushed;
perplexed, *but* not in despair; persecuted, *but* not
abandoned; struck down, *but* not destroyed. We always
carry around in our body the death of Jesus, so that the
life of Jesus may also be revealed in our body… So then,
death is at work in us, *but* life is at work in you.

It is written: "I believed; therefore I have spoken."
Since we have that same spirit of faith, we also believe
and therefore speak, because we know that the one who
raised the Lord Jesus from the dead will also raise us
with Jesus and present us with you to himself. All this is
for your benefit, so that the grace that is reaching more
and more people may cause thanksgiving to overflow to
the glory of God.

Therefore we do not lose heart. Though outwardly we
are wasting away, yet inwardly we are being renewed
day by day. For our light and momentary troubles are
achieving for us an eternal glory that far outweighs them
all. So we fix our eyes not on what is seen, but on what
is unseen, since what is seen is temporary, but what is
unseen is eternal.' *(Emphasis added.)*

2 Corinthians 5:1–5

'For we know that if the earthly tent we live in is
destroyed, we have a building from God, an eternal
house in heaven, not built by human hands. Meanwhile
we groan, longing to be clothed instead with our
heavenly dwelling, because when we are clothed, we will
not be found naked. For while we are in this tent, we
groan and are burdened, because we do not wish to be
unclothed but to be clothed instead with our heavenly
dwelling, so that what is mortal may be swallowed up
by life. Now the one who has fashioned us for this very

purpose is God, who has given us the Spirit as a deposit, guaranteeing what is to come.'

2 Corinthians 6:8–10

'genuine, *yet* regarded as impostors; known, *yet* regarded as unknown; dying, and *yet* we live on; beaten, and *yet* not killed; sorrowful, *yet* always rejoicing; poor, *yet* making many rich; having nothing, and *yet* possessing everything.' *(Emphasis added.)*

Session Focus

What we have in 2 Corinthians 4 is 'utterly butterly' Christianity: 'But… but… but… but'. Then in chapter 6, there is 'yeterly' Christianity: 'yet… yet… yet' (seven times!). Yes, we as Christians suffer like anyone else and often more so because of our faith, but it is the way we handle it by God's strength that so clearly transforms it into witness.

When we are in trying circumstances, we may be perplexed but we can go to a quiet place and lay the situation at His feet. There have been times when, as a bishop, I could see no way through a seemingly impossible situation, but after kneeling on the floor of my study with my staff team and telling God the problem, the answer would become clear. I have knelt and prayed with many people who were facing extreme difficulties but who proved the 'but God' truth: this is our God; we walk with Him. No problem is outside His power and wisdom.

It's a similar positive message with the 'yet' passage in chapter 6. As followers of Christ, we might feel devalued by the world, misunderstood by the world and burdened by a world without Christ; we might even suffer martyrdom. But then there is that wonderful summary: 'sorrowful, yet always rejoicing; poor, yet making many rich; having nothing, and yet possessing everything' (v10). Don't those words make your heart leap?

This triumphant faith is inspired by a passion for Christ; a passion that helps us say with Paul: 'I have been crucified with Christ and I no longer live, but Christ lives in me' (Gal. 2:20). As we identify more and more with the cross, as we deepen our grasp of Jesus' once and for all sacrifice, His suffering and His amazing love, so our petty baubles of importance fall through our fingers. To live for Christ increasingly becomes the motivation of our lives. Amy Carmichael, a missionary in India from 1895–1951, used attacks on her as a way of letting the light of Christ shine through her life.

I marvel at the witness of so many Christians who have used their suffering to glorify God. It is only natural to ask God to take away the suffering, but maybe we can add, as Jesus did, 'yet not my will, but yours be done' (Luke 22:42). More importantly, we can ask God how we can turn this suffering into a witness of His grace and love: for example, peace in our heart about our eternal destiny in Christ. Paul says, 'we know that the one who raised the Lord Jesus from the dead will also raise us with Jesus and present us with you to himself' (2 Cor. 4:14). Isn't that a beautiful expression of faith and peace? It is also a powerful stimulus for us to share our faith with others.

Typically, Paul now pushes the exciting truth outwards to 'more and more people' (v15). The evidence of what God was doing among His suffering servants – the great 'butterfly' evidence of grace – is news that spreads, news that encourages other believers and news that brings thanksgiving and that overflows (no trickle here!) to the glory of God. Yes, glory!

The last three verses of chapter 4 make me think of people looking at their mobile phones and not where they are going or taking in the scenery. Sometimes I want to say to those people, 'Look up!' But I want to say it even more to believers who look down in life rather than up. Verse 16 says that 'we are wasting away'. This is the uncomfortable truth, but instead of feeling downhearted, we are reminded that even in old age, the true believer needs time with God every day. Our troubles might not feel 'light and momentary' (v17) but when we look up, there is eternal glory ahead and we are encouraged to press on. Paul advises the Corinthians (and us) not to get bound up with earthly things as if that alone matters but to look up. What is seen will fade: the unseen is forever. It is a passage that particularly blesses those of us getting on in years – there is real life for Christian believers, even in old age!

Discussion Starters

1. What is meant by 'this treasure' (2 Cor. 4:7)? In what ways do we live as those who believe this is greater treasure than any earthly treasures? (See also Matt. 6:21.)

_____

_____

_____

_____

_____

2. Share about times when individuals have experienced suffering and subsequently God's all-surpassing power.

_____

_____

_____

_____

_____

3. What do you think is meant by: 'We always carry around in our body the death of Jesus, so that the life of Jesus may also be revealed in our body' (2 Cor. 4:10). How do we do this? Can we 'earth' its meaning into our lives?

_____

_____

_____

_____

_____

4. 'I believed; therefore I have spoken' (4:13). Invite some members of the group shared how they came to the same confident belief in Christ's resurrection and their own future resurrection and how it has emboldened their witness to Christ.

_____

_____

_____

_____

_____

5. It is said that our human bodies start decaying around the age of 22! What has helped members of the group, especially those in retirement years, to be renewed inwardly day by day (4:16)?

_____

_____

_____

_____

_____

6. Consider the seven 'yet' statements in 2 Corinthians 6:8–10. Share from your own life experiences, or those of others, the truth of these statements. If short of time, focus on the last three 'yets' (v10).

_____

_____

_____

_____

_____

Final Thoughts

Some people enjoy shopping for new clothes – others definitely don't! In heaven, we will not need to shop; we will be 'clothed instead with our heavenly dwelling' (2 Cor. 5:4), and we will hardly be able to contain our joy and excitement. Mortality will be swallowed by eternal life. Sufferings, disabilities, oppression and evil will be gone for ever. We will leave our temporary earthly tent and be welcomed into a 'building from God, an eternal house in heaven' (v1). Paul bursts with the expectation. I am greatly looking forward to it, as I am sure you are. But then comes the tension: we 'groan' (vv2,4); we want heaven now. We want perfect bodies now and we want a perfect environment now. But this is not God's plan for now. All that is reserved for heaven. We know from Revelation that in heaven we will never hunger or be thirsty but will be led by the lamb of God and 'God will wipe away every tear' (Rev. 7:17) from our eyes. Wonder of wonders, He has 'fashioned us for this very purpose' and given us the Spirit 'guaranteeing what is to come' (2 Cor. 5:5).

Closing Prayer

Lord Jesus, through Your Passion You brought us out of darkness into Your glorious light. Please forgive us when we fail to shine for You in this world. Please help us to have a burning passion for You, so that even in times of suffering, Your life may be revealed in our mortal bodies. Amen.

Further Reflection

Hopefully this study has strengthened you to be a better comforter and encourager, and to gently and clearly share God's Word. As you do this, may you be filled with Christ's love as messengers of the 'Father of compassion and the God of all comfort' (2 Cor. 1:3).

Serving with a passion for Christ our Saviour

'So we make it our goal to please him' (2 Cor. 5:9)

Icebreaker

Recall times in your life when you studied subjects that involved sitting an exam. In what ways were you affected by the pressure to do well? Compare those feelings with studying subjects, or learning a sport or hobby, where there was no exam at the end.

Opening Prayer

Lord Jesus, as today we think on the very heart of Your saving sacrifice for our sins, we pray that the Spirit will open up these truths with fresh depth and meaning for us all and that we may be renewed in our passion for You and in the giving of our lives as a living sacrifice in Your service. Amen.

Setting the Scene

Paul lifts our eyes to heaven several times in his second letter to the Corinthians, and he continues in chapter 5. We have that lovely phrase, 'away from the body and at home with the Lord' (2 Cor. 5:8), which is a far better description than 'death' or 'passed away'. I much prefer describing Christians whose earthly life has ended as 'having gone home'.

But now Paul bridges the gap between this life and the next by saying that our life's goal 'at home in the body or away from it' must be 'to please him' (v9). Is pleasing Christ your goal in life? The question is asked of all of us who love Him. When I was undergoing initial training in the army, we had a wonderful sergeant-major in charge of us. We loved him. He inspired us to do our very best, not for the army, but for him. So when it came to the day of our passing-out parade, we were distraught when, due to the strong wind, only those nearest to him heard his order to about turn; half of the parade went one way and half the other. We had let him down – on our passing-out parade. Paul urges us to do our best for Christ. And then he reminds us that we will all appear before His judgment seat, not in judgment of our salvation (verse 5 assures us about that), but how we have lived for Him and been His mouth, hands and feet in this fallen world. This is what spurs Paul on to 'try to persuade others' (v11) to love and serve God.

Bible Readings

2 Corinthians 5:6–10

'Therefore we are always confident and know that as long as we are at home in the body we are away from the Lord. For we live by faith, not by sight. We are confident, I say, and would prefer to be away from the body and at home with the Lord. So we make it our goal to please him, whether we are at home in the body or away from it. For we must all appear before the judgment seat of Christ, so that each of us may receive what is due to us for the things done while in the body, whether good or bad.'

2 Corinthians 5:11–15

'Since, then, we know what it is to fear the Lord, we try to persuade others. What we are is plain to God, and I hope it is also plain to your conscience. We are not trying to commend ourselves to you again, but are giving you an opportunity to take pride in us, so that you can answer those who take pride in what is seen rather than what is in the heart. If we are "out of our mind," as some say, it is for God; if we are in our right mind, it is for you. For Christ's love compels us, because we are convinced that one died for all, and therefore all died. And he died for all, that those who live should no longer live for themselves but for him who died for them and was raised again.'

2 Corinthians 5:16–21

'So from now on we regard no one from a worldly point of view. Though we once regarded Christ in this way, we do so no longer. Therefore, if anyone is in Christ, the new creation has come: the old has gone, the new is here! All this is from God, who reconciled us to himself through

Christ and gave us the ministry of reconciliation: that God was reconciling the world to himself in Christ, not counting people's sins against them. And he has committed to us the message of reconciliation. We are therefore Christ's ambassadors, as though God were making his appeal through us. We implore you on Christ's behalf: be reconciled to God. God made him who had no sin to be sin for us, so that in him we might become the righteousness of God.'

2 Corinthians 6:1–2

'As God's fellow workers we urge you not to receive God's grace in vain. For he says, "In the time of my favour I heard you, and in the day of salvation I helped you." I tell you, now is the time of God's favour, now is the day of salvation.'

Session Focus

In this final study session, we turn our attention to the cross and Paul's passionate outpouring about the gospel. The Corinthians seemed to think he is 'out of [his] mind' (2 Cor. 5:13) with the gospel he preached. So we can take some comfort when people think the same of us these days.

Paul's language shows the burning force in his heart: 'Christ's love compels us' (2 Cor. 5:14). The word 'compel' implies a situation where we are pressed in, such as canoeing down a river and suddenly entering a narrow gorge. Paul feels so compressed that he has no choice. This is because he is 'convinced' (v14) about the atonement. 'Convinced' means thought-through, examined and studied. He knew Christ's death was for the sins of the world. It is vital for our witness that we are convinced too.

That He 'died for all' (v14) does not mean all are saved but that salvation is now open to all who will respond in faith. This is the greatest gift we can ever receive but then Paul reminds us of the responsibility that comes with our salvation. We do not just sit and say 'Thank you'. We are no longer to live for ourselves first, looking after number one, but to live first for Christ who died and rose again.

Living for Christ requires us to evangelise. The phrase 'if anyone is in Christ, the new creation has come' (v17) means that once we are in Christ, our whole view of others changes; we begin to see our relatives, friends, colleagues and indeed everyone in the light of whether they are Christ's or not. I recall a young barrister sharing how, the morning after coming to faith, he started taking notice of others on the train and seeing them in the light of Christ, even praying for them. The Spirit had already changed his perspective.

Being a 'new creation' means we now see Christ differently (v16). While confirming Cambridge undergraduates some years ago, I asked each of them what Christ had meant to them before they came to faith. They all gave the usual answers: a prophet, a good teacher etc. Then I asked them what He meant to them now, and they each said, to the amazement of their unbelieving friends present in the service, 'He is my wonderful Saviour and Lord'. This is the result of being a 'new creation' – worship is transformed, our love and adoration is fired up, and our desire to make Him known is energised.

Verse 18 goes to the heart of the atonement: 'God… reconciled us to himself'. Sadly, many Christians see the word 'reconciliation' and immediately think it is about reconciliation between people. Yes, reconciliation between people is important, and it is throughout the Bible, but not here. In this passage, it is solely about reconciliation between humans and God. The cross dealt with sin and forgiveness so that we are no longer separated from God but brought back into fellowship with Him. Instead of being 'God's enemies' (Rom. 5:10), we have peace with God!

How can this wonderful truth be made known? Only through you and me, through believers. We alone are His ambassadors. Just as Britain's ambassadors kneel before the sovereign and receive their commission, we kneel before the King of kings and receive our commission. Verse 20 doesn't say *you* 'are therefore Christ's ambassadors', it says '*We* are therefore Christ's ambassadors' (my emphasis). It is the commission that the Corinthians, and we, must take up, imploring others 'on Christ's behalf: be reconciled to God' (v20). If Christians do not do so, no one else will.

Then comes one of the most profound verses in the Bible: 'God made him who had no sin to be sin for us' (v21). Not just bearing sins, He *became* sin. We shudder at what we can understand of the suffering of our Lord, but what it meant for Him to be separated from His Father, to cry, 'My God, my God, why have you forsaken me?' (Mark 15:34), to experience the darkness over Calvary and descent into Hades, goes beyond our human understanding. This is the depth of the Passion, which we remember on Good Friday. Why not take a minute or two to quietly reflect and worship the sacrificed lamb of God.

Discussion Starters

1. In 2 Corinthians 5:6, Paul says that 'we are always confident' regarding our eternal home-going. Discuss how you would help a Christian who lacks that confidence.

   _____

   _____

   _____

   _____

   _____

2. Discuss what Paul means by 'good or bad' (v10) things done while in our earthly bodies. How can we use our time on earth to please our heavenly Father?

   _____

   _____

   _____

   _____

   _____

3. If God judges by the heart, not by 'what is seen' (v12), then we should do the same. Think through the implications of this personally and for the local church.

   _____

   _____

   _____

   _____

   _____

4. Share your understanding of the amazing statement, 'he died for all' (v15), and what is means to you personally. Why it is vital for everybody to become convinced of this and respond?

   _____

   _____

   _____

   _____

   _____

5. Ask members of the group to share how their attitude to others and to Christ changed after becoming a Christian.

_____

_____

_____

_____

_____

6. How would you respond to the following question: 'I thought God loved everyone, so why do we need to be reconciled to Him?'

_____

_____

_____

_____

_____

7. Read verse 21 and discuss what it means that Jesus became 'to be sin for us'. How did His sacrifice ensure that 'we might become the righteousness of God'?

_____

_____

_____

_____

_____

Final Thoughts

It is a humbling and challenging statement that we are called 'God's fellow workers' (2 Cor. 6:1). We may recall the parable Jesus told of the two sons asked to work in the vineyard by their father (Matt. 21:28–32). One son said, 'I will', but did not do it; while the other said, 'I will not', but did do it. It is better to not promise at all than give a cheap, empty promise. The Corinthians were clearly reluctant to witness. They would probably find any excuse to put it off to another day. You can almost hear Paul shouting as he writes: 'now is the day of salvation' (v2). Today is always the day for sharing the good news of salvation.

Closing Prayer

Dearest Lord, Saviour of the world, we end our sessions in awe of Your amazing sacrifice in the Passion and Your defeat of sin and death. We pray that as we remember the events of Holy Week, we may understand more of what Your death and glorious resurrection really means, and respond more truly as those who can never thank You enough. We willingly offer You our lives for Your service with adoration and praise. Amen.

Further Reflection

The Corinthians withheld their affection from Paul (2 Cor. 6:12) but he opened his heart wide to them. He pleads with them to 'open wide your hearts also' (v13). May our hearts be always wide open to God and one another, and may we always be filled and fired with a passion for Christ.

Leader's Notes

General Notes

Everybody experiences suffering, so everybody has views on the subject. Why God allows suffering is the biggest block to belief by far. Tackling the subject through 2 Corinthians will hopefully give your group a biblical understanding of the true God, the God of compassion. In Paul's letter, we have insight into the Corinthians' false thinking on the matter as well as a rich exposition of the right way to look at it in Christ. As leader, try and keep the discussion focused on the session's topic rather than letting conversation drift.

As we proceed through the studies, Jesus becomes more and more central, with a wonderful focus on the cross for the last session. A useful resource to accompany your sessions is my book, *The One Big Question* (CWR, 2012), which tackles questions about suffering.

Music and collective sung worship have been life-long passions for me. With some sessions especially lending themselves to worship, you might find it helpful to have some singing at the start or close of your get-togethers. If your group would rather not sing, you could either play a song or read the words aloud. I have made some song suggestions for each study; some have words and/or music that I have written or composed, and some are by other hymn-writers or musicians. I hope that these will be able to benefit your time together as a group.

A great hymn to open any of the sessions is *Sing to God* (words: Timothy Dudley-Smith; music: Michael Baughen/ Jubilate Hymns).

STUDY ONE

Sharing in the sufferings of Christ

Song suggestions:
- *Man of sorrows* (Hillsong)
- *You never let go* (Matt Redman)
- *I lift my eyes to the quiet hills* (words: Timothy Dudley-Smith; music: Michael Baughen/Jubilate Hymns)

1. Many people would interpret the idea of God being loving or compassionate as meaning that He should take away all suffering like a divine grandfather, only there to please. However, the true God revealed to us in Christ is to be worshipped and loved. You might need to clarify that God is a God of compassion who suffered for us and with us.

2. In *The One Big Question* on pages 113–115 are experiences of cancer sufferers that give examples of how to comfort and how not to comfort.

3. Sharing Christ's suffering takes us to the heart of Lent and to the heart of Christ's Passion. Compare the accounts of Christ's sufferings in the Gospels with the list in 2 Corinthians 6:4–5. Broaden out the discussion to include suffering Christians across the world.

4. People in your group may have been in an environment (workplace, home or sports club) that was not particularly positive towards the Christian faith. It would be good to discuss people's experiences of witnessing in a heavily secular environment.

5. This could be a special devotional time.

6. The first question about lack of faith or unconfessed sin is very sensitive and you may not want to raise it. However, a lot of people are hurt by this sort of statement and you may

be able to bring the balm of God to a wounded soul in your group. You might find it helpful to stress that God is a God of comfort and compassion (2 Cor. 1:3).

7. No doubt some group members will major on healing but see if you can draw out wider concerns for prayer and God's response.

STUDY TWO

Seeking love in the Church of Christ

Song suggestions:
- *Build my life* (Housefires)
- *Lord of the cross* (words: Michael Saward; music: Michael Baughen/Jubilate Hymns)

This section of 2 Corinthians centres on being members of the Church and what that entails rather than concentrating on our personal Christian lives. Thankfully, the local church consists of all sorts of people: young and old, advocates of modern songs and those who prefer hymns, extroverts and introverts, men and women, intellectual and practical – and we are all called to love one another! Where possible, focus the discussion on the themes of love in the Church.

The Icebreaker could be fun but also a way of showing how we judge and form opinions that are wrong about others.

1. Holiness, in this context, means being a separate and special people, called to serve God with our lives (see Rom. 12:1–2).

2. Looking particularly at Ephesians 5:26, discuss how baptism, teaching of the Word and regular confession of faith, keep Christians cleansed and renewed. Draw out the picture of being the Bride and how we should be prepared for the Bridegroom – Jesus.

3. Widen the discussion out to loving action for the community. Quote 1 Thessalonians 3:12 where love is to 'overflow' in the Church and 'for everyone else'.

4. Emphasise the need to check the facts before one speaks, writes, emails or tweets words of criticism. Sadly, there have been times when I have received condemning letters from Christians who believed something about me that they read in the press. Even though I would write a reply, stating the true facts, quite often they would not want to resolve things, thus leaving a rift and a scar between us.

5. Although it is helpful to discuss how disagreement can become fractured, try not to let this become a personal grudge session.

6. This discussion starter is an ideal opportunity to stress how, as Christians, we have peace and assurance about our future, especially if there are enquirers present.

STUDY THREE

Spreading the aroma of Christ

Song suggestions:
- *For the sake of the world* (Brian Johnson, Joel Taylor, Jeremy Riddle; Bethel Music)
- *Christ Triumphant* (words: Michael Saward; music: Michael Baughen/Jubilate Hymns)

You might like to have a few scents, or invite members to bring their favourite scent, for the group to smell to stimulate the Icebreaker section, but it should work just as well without any.

As the Bible passages are being read, invite members to spot every mention of 'triumph', 'triumphal', 'victory' and 'conqueror'.

1. After a few minutes discussing this question, invite the group to look up Galatians 5:22–23 to read the list of the fruit of the Spirit.

2. If members of the group have not had any experience of people being unwelcoming, you could widen the discussion to consider Christians in non-Christian countries.

3. It might be worthwhile to draw out the truth of Colossians 2:13–15 to encourage those who are afraid of being known as a Christian as well as drawing out the day-to-day meaning of living in the triumph of Christ. You might like to briefly draw out what is the difference between a church living in the triumph of Christ and one being triumphalist.

4. A Christian who is uncertain about their eternal life might not be so concerned with evidence for the resurrection, but whether it includes them, so refer to scriptures such as John 3:16, Romans 6:4–5, 1 Corinthians 15:42–57 and Colossians 3:1–4.

STUDY FOUR

Shining with the light of Christ

Song suggestions:
• *Mighty to Save* (Hillsong)
• *Name of all majesty* (words: Timothy Dudley-Smith; music: Michael Baughen/Jubilate Hymns)

1. Draw out the blessings of the old covenant for the people of Israel, eg the Ten Commandments, the Psalms, the shared faith and how God delivered His people. However, it was all wrecked by disobedience, so a new covenant was needed, which would be a personal one as predicted in Jeremiah 31:33–34. When we receive the wine during Communion, we receive and renew our acceptance of

a personal covenant of love. The wine symbolises the blood that sealed the new covenant just as blood sealed the old covenant.

2. The group might mention pride, peer pressure or poor teaching as times when they resisted God. (See 1 John 2:9–11.)

3. When discussing how we 'contemplate the Lord's glory', encourage a wide range of responses, which might include the Word of God, creation (Psa. 19), great paintings or inspirational music. You might want to refer to Isaiah 6:1–4.

4. While good to discuss unhelpful teaching, members of your group might take differing views on what constitutes a distortion of the Word of God. Try and maintain an open discussion by focusing on the positives of sharing the good news.

5. Which biblical truths to share, and how to do so, will hopefully stir up useful debate.

6. When thinking about how to give glory to God, you might want to look up Revelation 4:11; 5:12–13; 7:11–12 and draw out the reasons for the glorifying. Invite the group to share their favourite ways of praising and glorifying God, eg songs and hymns etc.

7. 2 Corinthians 4:6 is a verse bathing in spiritual wonder and joy. It would be great if your group could capture that sense and end the session on a Christ-glorifying 'high'! You might decide to look at Final Thoughts first before discussing this question.

STUDY FIVE

Showing the life of Jesus in our mortal bodies

Song suggestions:
- *Resurrecting* (Elevation Worship)
- *As the deer longs for water* (words and music: Michael Baughen/Jubilate Hymns)

1. The meaning of 'this treasure' (2 Cor. 4:7) is God shining into our hearts. You might like to also refer to Matthew 13:44–46. Heavenly treasure is worth more than anything else in the world. Does the Church need to challenge the human focus on earthly treasure?

2. This question follows on from the Icebreaker about long-term illness or disability. As well as discussing personal experiences, you could talk about Christians suffering throughout the world. (You might like to search online or look in Christian magazines for inspiring testimonies.)

3. When thinking about how we can reveal the life of Christ in our bodies, you might want to look up Galatians 2:20 and discuss how being crucified with Christ also means that 'Christ lives in me'. You could also look at how immersion baptism signifies death to the old and resurrection to new life. Other helpful verses are Luke 9:23: 'Whoever wants to be my disciple must deny themselves and take up their cross daily'. And 1 Peter 2:24: '"He himself bore our sins" in his body on the cross, so that we might die to sins and live for righteousness'.

4. Discuss evidences for Christ's resurrection: the empty tomb, the transformation of the disciples, the large number of witnesses and so on. Look up 1 Corinthians 15:20–23 regarding our own resurrection.

5. Discuss the benefits of having a regular pattern of devotional reading and prayer. Hopefully there will be a variety of responses about what has really helped members to be renewed every day.

6. Our experiences of suffering won't be the same as Paul's, but discuss the contrast between our response to suffering and the world's response to suffering. You might like to close the session by looking again at 2 Corinthians 6:10.

STUDY SIX

Serving with a passion for Christ our Saviour

Song suggestions:
- *I will offer up my life* (Matt Redman)
- *When I survey the wondrous cross* (words: Isaac Watts)
- *Go forth and tell* (words: Jim Seddon; music: Michael Baughen/Jubilate Hymns)

1. The phrase 'we are always confident' (2 Cor. 5:6) follows Paul's reminder that God has 'given us the Spirit as a deposit' (v5); you might find it helpful to focus on this aspect. It is also worth emphasising that many people hear well-known verses like John 3:16 without receiving the Spirit's affirmation. Explain how many of us need to ask God to make Himself real in our hearts. Fiona Castle tells a powerful story of how she developed a personal relationship with Christ in her book *No Flowers... Just Lots of Joy* (Kingsway Publications, 1996).

2. Discuss common attitudes to those who are poor, wealthy, of other ethnic origins, mentally disabled and so on. Contrast the amount of time spent improving our bodies with the time spent improving our souls.

3. As leader, you may want to offer an example of this in your own life – where you perhaps you may have misjudged someone based on visible factors, and then been happily proved wrong.

4. Spend some time going over why Christ's death needed to happen and how we are saved through it. To help understand the concept of sacrifice, you might like to reference Leviticus 3:1–2 and Hebrews 9:26–28. Be sure to draw out personal testimony to the glorious truth that Jesus 'died for all' (2 Cor. 5:15).

5. Discussion of how attitudes change after becoming a Christian might naturally lead to a time of prayer for friends and loved ones who do not yet know Christ personally.

6. Read Romans 5:6–11, which describes us as sinners and enemies of God, but then follow with Romans 5:1 to underline how God has made it possible for us to have peace with Him. Again, focus the discussion on the wonder of a personal relationship with God.

7. You might like to look up Galatians 3:13: 'Christ redeemed us from the curse of the law by becoming a curse for us'. When Jesus took on our sin, He became cursed. His death paid for (redeemed) our sin so that we could become right with God.

If your sessions finish just before Holy Week begins, you might like to read Isaiah 53:5–6 as an appropriate ending to the studies.

Notes...

Notes...

Be inspired by God.
Every day.

Confidently face life's challenges by equipping yourself daily with God's Word. There is something for everyone...

Every Day with Jesus

Selwyn Hughes' renowned writing is updated by Mick Brooks into these trusted and popular notes.

Life Every Day

Jeff Lucas helps apply the Bible to daily life with his trademark humour and insight.

Inspiring Women
Every Day

Encouragement, uplifting scriptures and insightful daily thoughts for women.

The Manual

Straight-talking guides to help men walk daily with God. Written by Carl Beech.

To find out more about all our daily Bible reading notes, or to take out a subscription, visit **cwr.org.uk/biblenotes** or call **01252 784700**.
Also available in Christian bookshops.

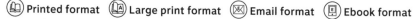 Printed format Large print format Email format Ebook format

SmallGroup central

All of our small group ideas and resources in one place

Online:

smallgroupcentral.org.uk
is filled with free video teaching, tools, articles and a whole host of ideas.

On the road:

A range of seminars themed for small groups can be brought to your local community. Contact us at **hello@smallgroupcentral.org.uk**

In print:

Books, study guides and DVDs covering an extensive list of themes, Bible books and life issues.

Find out more at:
smallgroupcentral.org.uk

Courses and events

Waverley Abbey College

Publishing and media

Conference facilities

Transforming lives

CWR's vision is to enable people to experience personal transformation through applying God's Word to their lives and relationships.

Our Bible-based training and resources help people around the world to:
• Grow in their walk with God
• Understand and apply Scripture to their lives
• Resource themselves and their church
• Develop pastoral care and counselling skills
• Train for leadership
• Strengthen relationships, marriage and family life and much more.

Our insightful writers provide daily Bible reading notes and other resources for all ages, and our experienced course designers and presenters have gained an international reputation for excellence and effectiveness.

CWR's Training and Conference Centre in Surrey, England, provides excellent facilities in an idyllic setting - ideal for both learning and spiritual refreshment.

CWR Applying God's Word
to everyday life and relationships

CWR, Waverley Abbey House,
Waverley Lane, Farnham,
Surrey GU9 8EP, UK

Telephone: **+44 (0)1252 784700**
Email: **info@cwr.org.uk**
Website: **cwr.org.uk**

Registered Charity No. 294387
Company Registration No. 1990308